MY PET
SNAIL LOGBOOK

THIS BOOK BELONGS TO:

....

....

ABOUT YOUR PET

NICKNAME

GENUS

AGE

SEX

SPECIES

CHARACTERTICS

HABITAT

ABOUT SNAIL

LIFE SPAN • 2-7 Years

SIZE • A few centimeters to 12 inches

DIET • Fruit, veggies and calcium

TEMPERATURE • 19-25°C (66-77 °F)

MEDICATION

MEDICATION	DATE:	NOTES:

GROWTH CHART

DATE	WEIGHT	NOTES

GROWTH CHART

DATE	WEIGHT	NOTES

MY PET SNAIL
DAILY ACTIVITY

WEEK OF .... DATE ....

SUN MON TUE WED THU FRI SUN

	Activity	S	M	T	W	T	F	S
	Feed snail	○	○	○	○	○	○	○
	Fresh water	○	○	○	○	○	○	○
	Check a calcium source	○	○	○	○	○	○	○
	Remove poop	○	○	○	○	○	○	○
	Remove rotting food	○	○	○	○	○	○	○
	Spray the tank with water.	○	○	○	○	○	○	○
	Check the temperature	○	○	○	○	○	○	○

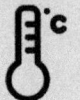

HIGHLY OF THE WEEK:

MY PET SNAIL

WEEKLY ACTIVITY

WEEK OF..........................
DATE..............................

- Wash snail's shell
- Weigh snail and record
- Wipe tank sides and lid
- Wash cuttle fish bone if dirty

FEW MONTHLY ACTIVITY

- Top up substrate
- Wash & top up moss

TO DO
1.
2.
3.
4.
5.
6.

SHOPPING LIST

NOTES:

MY PET SNAIL
DAILY ACTIVITY

WEEK OF .... DATE............................

SUN MON TUE WED THU FRI SUN

Activity	SUN	MON	TUE	WED	THU	FRI	SUN
Feed snail	○	○	○	○	○	○	○
Fresh water	○	○	○	○	○	○	○
Check a calcium source	○	○	○	○	○	○	○
Remove poop	○	○	○	○	○	○	○
Remove rotting food	○	○	○	○	○	○	○
Spray the tank with water.	○	○	○	○	○	○	○
Check the temperature	○	○	○	○	○	○	○

HIGHLY OF THE WEEK:

MY PET SNAIL
WEEKLY ACTIVITY

WEEK OF..........................
DATE..............................

- Wash snail's shell
- Weigh snail and record
- Wipe tank sides and lid
- Wash cuttle fish bone if dirty

FEW MONTHLY ACTIVITY

- Top up substrate
- Wash & top up moss

TO DO
1.
2.
3.
4.
5.
6.

SHOPPING LIST

NOTES:

MY PET SNAIL
DAILY ACTIVITY

WEEK OF .... DATE...........................

SUN MON TUE WED THU FRI SUN

Activity	
Feed snail	● ● ● ● ● ● ●
Fresh water	● ● ● ● ● ● ●
Check a calcium source	● ● ● ● ● ● ●
Remove poop	● ● ● ● ● ● ●
Remove rotting food	● ● ● ● ● ● ●
Spray the tank with water.	● ● ● ● ● ● ●
Check the temperature	● ● ● ● ● ● ●

HIGHLY OF THE WEEK:

MY PET SNAIL
WEEKLY ACTIVITY

WEEK OF..........................
DATE..............................

- Wash snail's shell
- Weigh snail and record
- Wipe tank sides and lid
- Wash cuttle fish bone if dirty

FEW MONTHLY ACTIVITY

- Top up substrate
- Wash & top up moss

TO DO
1.
2.
3.
4.
5.
6.

SHOPPING LIST

NOTES:

MY PET SNAIL
DAILY ACTIVITY

WEEK OF .... DATE ....

SUN MON TUE WED THU FRI SUN

- Feed snail
- Fresh water
- Check a calcium source
- Remove poop
- Remove rotting food
- Spray the tank with water.
- Check the temperature

HIGHLY OF THE WEEK:

MY PET SNAIL
WEEKLY ACTIVITY

WEEK OF..........................
DATE..............................

- Wash snail's shell
- Weigh snail and record
- Wipe tank sides and lid
- Wash cuttle fish bone if dirty

FEW MONTHLY ACTIVITY

- Top up substrate
- Wash & top up moss

TO DO
1.
2.
3.
4.
5.
6.

SHOPPING LIST

NOTES:

MY PET SNAIL
DAILY ACTIVITY

WEEK OF .... DATE ....

SUN MON TUE WED THU FRI SUN

	Feed snail	○ ○ ○ ○ ○ ○ ○
	Fresh water	○ ○ ○ ○ ○ ○ ○
	Check a calcium source	○ ○ ○ ○ ○ ○ ○
	Remove poop	○ ○ ○ ○ ○ ○ ○
	Remove rotting food	○ ○ ○ ○ ○ ○ ○
	Spray the tank with water.	○ ○ ○ ○ ○ ○ ○
	Check the temperature	○ ○ ○ ○ ○ ○ ○

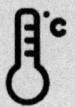

HIGHLY OF THE WEEK:

MY PET SNAIL

WEEKLY ACTIVITY

WEEK OF..........................
DATE..............................

- Wash snail's shell
- Weigh snail and record
- Wipe tank sides and lid
- Wash cuttle fish bone if dirty

FEW MONTHLY ACTIVITY

- Top up substrate
- Wash & top up moss

TO DO
1.
2.
3.
4.
5.
6.

SHOPPING LIST

NOTES:

MY PET SNAIL
DAILY ACTIVITY

WEEK OF .... DATE ....

SUN MON TUE WED THU FRI SUN

- Feed snail
- Fresh water
- Check a calcium source
- Remove poop
- Remove rotting food
- Spray the tank with water.
- Check the temperature

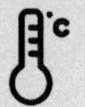

HIGHLY OF THE WEEK:

MY PET SNAIL
WEEKLY ACTIVITY

WEEK OF..........................
DATE..............................

- Wash snail's shell
- Weigh snail and record
- Wipe tank sides and lid
- Wash cuttle fish bone if dirty

FEW MONTHLY ACTIVITY

- Top up substrate
- Wash & top up moss

TO DO
1.
2.
3.
4.
5.
6.

SHOPPING LIST

NOTES:

MY PET SNAIL
DAILY ACTIVITY

WEEK OF .... DATE ....

SUN MON TUE WED THU FRI SUN

- Feed snail
- Fresh water
- Check a calcium source
- Remove poop
- Remove rotting food
- Spray the tank with water.
- Check the temperature

HIGHLY OF THE WEEK:

MY PET SNAIL

WEEK OF..........................
DATE...............................

WEEKLY ACTIVITY

- Wash snail's shell
- Weigh snail and record
- Wipe tank sides and lid
- Wash cuttle fish bone if dirty

FEW MONTHLY ACTIVITY

- Top up substrate
- Wash & top up moss

TO DO
1.
2.
3.
4.
5.
6.

SHOPPING LIST

NOTES:

MY PET SNAIL
DAILY ACTIVITY

WEEK OF .... DATE..........................

	SUN	MON	TUE	WED	THU	FRI	SUN
Feed snail	○	○	○	○	○	○	○
Fresh water	○	○	○	○	○	○	○
Check a calcium source	○	○	○	○	○	○	○
Remove poop	○	○	○	○	○	○	○
Remove rotting food	○	○	○	○	○	○	○
Spray the tank with water.	○	○	○	○	○	○	○
Check the temperature	○	○	○	○	○	○	○

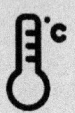

HIGHLY OF THE WEEK:

MY PET SNAIL
WEEKLY ACTIVITY

WEEK OF..........................
DATE..............................

- Wash snail's shell
- Weigh snail and record
- Wipe tank sides and lid
- Wash cuttle fish bone if dirty

FEW MONTHLY ACTIVITY

- Top up substrate
- Wash & top up moss

TO DO
1.
2.
3.
4.
5.
6.

SHOPPING LIST

NOTES:

MY PET SNAIL
DAILY ACTIVITY

WEEK OF .... DATE..........................
SUN MON TUE WED THU FRI SUN

	Feed snail	○ ○ ○ ○ ○ ○ ○
	Fresh water	○ ○ ○ ○ ○ ○ ○
	Check a calcium source	○ ○ ○ ○ ○ ○ ○
	Remove poop	○ ○ ○ ○ ○ ○ ○
	Remove rotting food	○ ○ ○ ○ ○ ○ ○
	Spray the tank with water.	○ ○ ○ ○ ○ ○ ○
	Check the temperature	○ ○ ○ ○ ○ ○ ○

HIGHLY OF THE WEEK:

MY PET SNAIL
WEEKLY ACTIVITY

WEEK OF..........................
DATE..............................

- Wash snail's shell
- Weigh snail and record
- Wipe tank sides and lid
- Wash cuttle fish bone if dirty

FEW MONTHLY ACTIVITY

- Top up substrate
- Wash & top up moss

TO DO
1.
2.
3.
4.
5.
6.

SHOPPING LIST

NOTES:

MY PET SNAIL
DAILY ACTIVITY

WEEK OF .... DATE ....

	SUN	MON	TUE	WED	THU	FRI	SUN
Feed snail	○	○	○	○	○	○	○
Fresh water	○	○	○	○	○	○	○
Check a calcium source	○	○	○	○	○	○	○
Remove poop	○	○	○	○	○	○	○
Remove rotting food	○	○	○	○	○	○	○
Spray the tank with water.	○	○	○	○	○	○	○
Check the temperature	○	○	○	○	○	○	○

HIGHLY OF THE WEEK:

MY PET SNAIL
WEEKLY ACTIVITY

WEEK OF..........................
DATE..............................

- Wash snail's shell
- Weigh snail and record
- Wipe tank sides and lid
- Wash cuttle fish bone if dirty

FEW MONTHLY ACTIVITY

- Top up substrate
- Wash & top up moss

TO DO
1.
2.
3.
4.
5.
6.

SHOPPING LIST

NOTES:

MY PET SNAIL
DAILY ACTIVITY

WEEK OF .... DATE............................

SUN MON TUE WED THU FRI SUN

- Feed snail ○ ○ ○ ○ ○ ○ ○
- Fresh water ○ ○ ○ ○ ○ ○ ○
- Check a calcium source ○ ○ ○ ○ ○ ○ ○
- Remove poop ○ ○ ○ ○ ○ ○ ○
- Remove rotting food ○ ○ ○ ○ ○ ○ ○
- Spray the tank with water. ○ ○ ○ ○ ○ ○ ○
- Check the temperature ○ ○ ○ ○ ○ ○ ○

HIGHLY OF THE WEEK:

MY PET SNAIL
WEEKLY ACTIVITY

WEEK OF..........................
DATE.................................

- Wash snail's shell
- Weigh snail and record
- Wipe tank sides and lid
- Wash cuttle fish bone if dirty

FEW MONTHLY ACTIVITY

- Top up substrate
- Wash & top up moss

TO DO
1.
2.
3.
4.
5.
6.

SHOPPING LIST

NOTES:

MY PET SNAIL
DAILY ACTIVITY

WEEK OF .... DATE ....

SUN MON TUE WED THU FRI SUN

🍎	Feed snail	● ● ● ● ● ● ●
💧	Fresh water	● ● ● ● ● ● ●
Ca	Check a calcium source	● ● ● ● ● ● ●
💩	Remove poop	● ● ● ● ● ● ●
	Remove rotting food	● ● ● ● ● ● ●
	Spray the tank with water.	● ● ● ● ● ● ●
°C	Check the temperature	● ● ● ● ● ● ●

HIGHLY OF THE WEEK:

MY PET SNAIL
WEEKLY ACTIVITY

WEEK OF..........................
DATE.............................

- Wash snail's shell
- Weigh snail and record
- Wipe tank sides and lid
- Wash cuttle fish bone if dirty

FEW MONTHLY ACTIVITY

- Top up substrate
- Wash & top up moss

TO DO
1.
2.
3.
4.
5.
6.

SHOPPING LIST

NOTES:

MY PET SNAIL
DAILY ACTIVITY

WEEK OF .... DATE..........................
SUN MON TUE WED THU FRI SUN

- Feed snail
- Fresh water
- Check a calcium source
- Remove poop
- Remove rotting food
- Spray the tank with water.
- Check the temperature

HIGHLY OF THE WEEK:

MY PET SNAIL
WEEKLY ACTIVITY

WEEK OF..........................
DATE................................

- Wash snail's shell
- Weigh snail and record
- Wipe tank sides and lid
- Wash cuttle fish bone if dirty

FEW MONTHLY ACTIVITY

- Top up substrate
- Wash & top up moss

TO DO
1.
2.
3.
4.
5.
6.

SHOPPING LIST

NOTES:

MY PET SNAIL
DAILY ACTIVITY

WEEK OF .... DATE.............................

SUN MON TUE WED THU FRI SUN

	Activity	S	M	T	W	T	F	S
	Feed snail	○	○	○	○	○	○	○
	Fresh water	○	○	○	○	○	○	○
	Check a calcium source	○	○	○	○	○	○	○
	Remove poop	○	○	○	○	○	○	○
	Remove rotting food	○	○	○	○	○	○	○
	Spray the tank with water.	○	○	○	○	○	○	○
	Check the temperature	○	○	○	○	○	○	○

HIGHLY OF THE WEEK:

MY PET SNAIL
WEEKLY ACTIVITY

WEEK OF..........................
DATE..............................

- Wash snail's shell
- Weigh snail and record
- Wipe tank sides and lid
- Wash cuttle fish bone if dirty

FEW MONTHLY ACTIVITY

- Top up substrate
- Wash & top up moss

TO DO
1.
2.
3.
4.
5.
6.

SHOPPING LIST

NOTES:

MY PET SNAIL
DAILY ACTIVITY

WEEK OF .... DATE............................

SUN MON TUE WED THU FRI SUN

	Feed snail	● ● ● ● ● ● ●
	Fresh water	● ● ● ● ● ● ●
	Check a calcium source	● ● ● ● ● ● ●
	Remove poop	● ● ● ● ● ● ●
	Remove rotting food	● ● ● ● ● ● ●
	Spray the tank with water.	● ● ● ● ● ● ●
	Check the temperature	● ● ● ● ● ● ●

HIGHLY OF THE WEEK:

MY PET SNAIL
WEEKLY ACTIVITY

WEEK OF.........................
DATE.............................

- Wash snail's shell
- Weigh snail and record
- Wipe tank sides and lid
- Wash cuttle fish bone if dirty

FEW MONTHLY ACTIVITY

- Top up substrate
- Wash & top up moss

TO DO
1.
2.
3.
4.
5.
6.

SHOPPING LIST

NOTES:

MY PET SNAIL
DAILY ACTIVITY

WEEK OF .... DATE ....

SUN MON TUE WED THU FRI SUN

- Feed snail
- Fresh water
- Check a calcium source
- Remove poop
- Remove rotting food
- Spray the tank with water.
- Check the temperature

HIGHLY OF THE WEEK:

MY PET SNAIL
WEEKLY ACTIVITY

WEEK OF..........................
DATE................................

- Wash snail's shell
- Weigh snail and record
- Wipe tank sides and lid
- Wash cuttle fish bone if dirty

FEW MONTHLY ACTIVITY

- Top up substrate
- Wash & top up moss

TO DO
1.
2.
3.
4.
5.
6.

SHOPPING LIST

NOTES:

MY PET SNAIL
DAILY ACTIVITY

WEEK OF .... DATE ....

SUN MON TUE WED THU FRI SUN

	Activity	SUN	MON	TUE	WED	THU	FRI	SUN
	Feed snail	○	○	○	○	○	○	○
	Fresh water	○	○	○	○	○	○	○
	Check a calcium source	○	○	○	○	○	○	○
	Remove poop	○	○	○	○	○	○	○
	Remove rotting food	○	○	○	○	○	○	○
	Spray the tank with water.	○	○	○	○	○	○	○
	Check the temperature	○	○	○	○	○	○	○

HIGHLY OF THE WEEK:

MY PET SNAIL

WEEK OF..........................
DATE..............................

WEEKLY ACTIVITY

- Wash snail's shell
- Weigh snail and record
- Wipe tank sides and lid
- Wash cuttle fish bone if dirty

FEW MONTHLY ACTIVITY

- Top up substrate
- Wash & top up moss

TO DO
1.
2.
3.
4.
5.
6.

SHOPPING LIST

NOTES:

MY PET SNAIL
DAILY ACTIVITY

WEEK OF .... DATE..........................

SUN MON TUE WED THU FRI SUN

- Feed snail
- Fresh water
- Check a calcium source
- Remove poop
- Remove rotting food
- Spray the tank with water.
- Check the temperature

HIGHLY OF THE WEEK:

MY PET SNAIL
WEEKLY ACTIVITY

WEEK OF.........................
DATE.............................

- Wash snail's shell
- Weigh snail and record
- Wipe tank sides and lid
- Wash cuttle fish bone if dirty

FEW MONTHLY ACTIVITY

- Top up substrate
- Wash & top up moss

TO DO
1.
2.
3.
4.
5.
6.

SHOPPING LIST

NOTES:

MY PET SNAIL
DAILY ACTIVITY

WEEK OF .... DATE..........................
SUN MON TUE WED THU FRI SUN

- Feed snail
- Fresh water
- Check a calcium source
- Remove poop
- Remove rotting food
- Spray the tank with water.
- Check the temperature

HIGHLY OF THE WEEK:

MY PET SNAIL
WEEKLY ACTIVITY

WEEK OF..........................
DATE................................

- Wash snail's shell
- Weigh snail and record
- Wipe tank sides and lid
- Wash cuttle fish bone if dirty

FEW MONTHLY ACTIVITY

- Top up substrate
- Wash & top up moss

TO DO
1.
2.
3.
4.
5.
6.

SHOPPING LIST

NOTES:

MY PET SNAIL
DAILY ACTIVITY

WEEK OF .... DATE..........................
SUN MON TUE WED THU FRI SUN

	Activity	SUN	MON	TUE	WED	THU	FRI	SUN
	Feed snail	○	○	○	○	○	○	○
	Fresh water	○	○	○	○	○	○	○
	Check a calcium source	○	○	○	○	○	○	○
	Remove poop	○	○	○	○	○	○	○
	Remove rotting food	○	○	○	○	○	○	○
	Spray the tank with water.	○	○	○	○	○	○	○
	Check the temperature	○	○	○	○	○	○	○

HIGHLY OF THE WEEK:

MY PET SNAIL
WEEKLY ACTIVITY

WEEK OF..........................
DATE..............................

- Wash snail's shell
- Weigh snail and record
- Wipe tank sides and lid
- Wash cuttle fish bone if dirty

FEW MONTHLY ACTIVITY

- Top up substrate
- Wash & top up moss

TO DO
1.
2.
3.
4.
5.
6.

SHOPPING LIST

NOTES:

MY PET SNAIL
DAILY ACTIVITY

WEEK OF .... DATE ....

SUN MON TUE WED THU FRI SUN

Feed snail ○ ○ ○ ○ ○ ○ ○

Fresh water ○ ○ ○ ○ ○ ○ ○

Check a calcium source ○ ○ ○ ○ ○ ○ ○

Remove poop ○ ○ ○ ○ ○ ○ ○

Remove rotting food ○ ○ ○ ○ ○ ○ ○

Spray the tank with water. ○ ○ ○ ○ ○ ○ ○

Check the temperature ○ ○ ○ ○ ○ ○ ○

HIGHLY OF THE WEEK:

MY PET SNAIL
WEEKLY ACTIVITY

WEEK OF..........................
DATE..............................

- Wash snail's shell
- Weigh snail and record
- Wipe tank sides and lid
- Wash cuttle fish bone if dirty

FEW MONTHLY ACTIVITY

- Top up substrate
- Wash & top up moss

TO DO
1.
2.
3.
4.
5.
6.

SHOPPING LIST

NOTES:

MY PET SNAIL
DAILY ACTIVITY

WEEK OF .... DATE ....

SUN MON TUE WED THU FRI SUN

- Feed snail
- Fresh water
- Check a calcium source
- Remove poop
- Remove rotting food
- Spray the tank with water.
- Check the temperature

HIGHLY OF THE WEEK:

MY PET SNAIL
WEEKLY ACTIVITY

WEEK OF..........................
DATE..............................

- Wash snail's shell
- Weigh snail and record
- Wipe tank sides and lid
- Wash cuttle fish bone if dirty

FEW MONTHLY ACTIVITY

- Top up substrate
- Wash & top up moss

TO DO
1.
2.
3.
4.
5.
6.

SHOPPING LIST

NOTES:

MY PET SNAIL
DAILY ACTIVITY

WEEK OF ……… DATE………………………

SUN MON TUE WED THU FRI SUN

- Feed snail
- Fresh water
- Check a calcium source
- Remove poop
- Remove rotting food
- Spray the tank with water.
- Check the temperature

HIGHLY OF THE WEEK:

MY PET SNAIL
WEEKLY ACTIVITY

WEEK OF..........................
DATE..............................

- Wash snail's shell
- Weigh snail and record
- Wipe tank sides and lid
- Wash cuttle fish bone if dirty

FEW MONTHLY ACTIVITY

- Top up substrate
- Wash & top up moss

TO DO
1.
2.
3.
4.
5.
6.

SHOPPING LIST

NOTES:

MY PET SNAIL
DAILY ACTIVITY

WEEK OF .... DATE..........................
SUN MON TUE WED THU FRI SUN

- Feed snail
- Fresh water
- Check a calcium source
- Remove poop
- Remove rotting food
- Spray the tank with water.
- Check the temperature

HIGHLY OF THE WEEK:

MY PET SNAIL
WEEKLY ACTIVITY

WEEK OF..........................
DATE..............................

- Wash snail's shell
- Weigh snail and record
- Wipe tank sides and lid
- Wash cuttle fish bone if dirty

FEW MONTHLY ACTIVITY

- Top up substrate
- Wash & top up moss

TO DO
1.
2.
3.
4.
5.
6.

SHOPPING LIST

NOTES:

MY PET SNAIL
DAILY ACTIVITY

WEEK OF .... DATE ....

SUN MON TUE WED THU FRI SUN

- Feed snail
- Fresh water
- Check a calcium source
- Remove poop
- Remove rotting food
- Spray the tank with water.
- Check the temperature

HIGHLY OF THE WEEK:

MY PET SNAIL
WEEKLY ACTIVITY

WEEK OF..........................
DATE..............................

- Wash snail's shell
- Weigh snail and record
- Wipe tank sides and lid
- Wash cuttle fish bone if dirty

FEW MONTHLY ACTIVITY

- Top up substrate
- Wash & top up moss

TO DO
1.
2.
3.
4.
5.
6.

SHOPPING LIST

NOTES:

MY PET SNAIL
DAILY ACTIVITY

WEEK OF .... DATE..........................

SUN MON TUE WED THU FRI SUN

Feed snail	○ ○ ○ ○ ○ ○ ○
Fresh water	○ ○ ○ ○ ○ ○ ○
Check a calcium source	○ ○ ○ ○ ○ ○ ○
Remove poop	○ ○ ○ ○ ○ ○ ○
Remove rotting food	○ ○ ○ ○ ○ ○ ○
Spray the tank with water.	○ ○ ○ ○ ○ ○ ○
Check the temperature	○ ○ ○ ○ ○ ○ ○

HIGHLY OF THE WEEK:

MY PET SNAIL
WEEKLY ACTIVITY

WEEK OF..........................
DATE..............................

- Wash snail's shell
- Weigh snail and record
- Wipe tank sides and lid
- Wash cuttle fish bone if dirty

FEW MONTHLY ACTIVITY

- Top up substrate
- Wash & top up moss

TO DO
1.
2.
3.
4.
5.
6.

SHOPPING LIST

NOTES:

MY PET SNAIL
DAILY ACTIVITY

WEEK OF .... DATE..........................

SUN MON TUE WED THU FRI SUN

- Feed snail
- Fresh water
- Check a calcium source
- Remove poop
- Remove rotting food
- Spray the tank with water.
- Check the temperature

HIGHLY OF THE WEEK:

MY PET SNAIL
WEEKLY ACTIVITY

WEEK OF..........................
DATE..............................

- Wash snail's shell
- Weigh snail and record
- Wipe tank sides and lid
- Wash cuttle fish bone if dirty

FEW MONTHLY ACTIVITY

- Top up substrate
- Wash & top up moss

TO DO
1.
2.
3.
4.
5.
6.

SHOPPING LIST

NOTES:

# MY PET SNAIL
DAILY ACTIVITY

WEEK OF .... DATE..........................
SUN MON TUE WED THU FRI SUN

	Activity	S	M	T	W	T	F	S
	Feed snail	○	○	○	○	○	○	○
	Fresh water	○	○	○	○	○	○	○
	Check a calcium source	○	○	○	○	○	○	○
	Remove poop	○	○	○	○	○	○	○
	Remove rotting food	○	○	○	○	○	○	○
	Spray the tank with water.	○	○	○	○	○	○	○
	Check the temperature	○	○	○	○	○	○	○

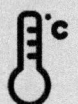

HIGHLY OF THE WEEK:

MY PET SNAIL
WEEKLY ACTIVITY

WEEK OF..........................
DATE..............................

- Wash snail's shell
- Weigh snail and record
- Wipe tank sides and lid
- Wash cuttle fish bone if dirty

FEW MONTHLY ACTIVITY

- Top up substrate
- Wash & top up moss

TO DO
1.
2.
3.
4.
5.
6.

SHOPPING LIST

NOTES:

MY PET SNAIL
DAILY ACTIVITY

WEEK OF .... DATE..........................

SUN MON TUE WED THU FRI SUN

	Activity	
	Feed snail	○ ○ ○ ○ ○ ○ ○
	Fresh water	○ ○ ○ ○ ○ ○ ○
	Check a calcium source	○ ○ ○ ○ ○ ○ ○
	Remove poop	○ ○ ○ ○ ○ ○ ○
	Remove rotting food	○ ○ ○ ○ ○ ○ ○
	Spray the tank with water.	○ ○ ○ ○ ○ ○ ○
	Check the temperature	○ ○ ○ ○ ○ ○ ○

HIGHLY OF THE WEEK:

MY PET SNAIL

WEEKLY ACTIVITY

WEEK OF..........................
DATE..............................

- Wash snail's shell
- Weigh snail and record
- Wipe tank sides and lid
- Wash cuttle fish bone if dirty

FEW MONTHLY ACTIVITY

- Top up substrate
- Wash & top up moss

TO DO
1.
2.
3.
4.
5.
6.

SHOPPING LIST

NOTES:

MY PET SNAIL
DAILY ACTIVITY

WEEK OF .... DATE ....

		SUN	MON	TUE	WED	THU	FRI	SUN
	Feed snail	○	○	○	○	○	○	○
	Fresh water	○	○	○	○	○	○	○
	Check a calcium source	○	○	○	○	○	○	○
	Remove poop	○	○	○	○	○	○	○
	Remove rotting food	○	○	○	○	○	○	○
	Spray the tank with water.	○	○	○	○	○	○	○
	Check the temperature	○	○	○	○	○	○	○

HIGHLY OF THE WEEK:

MY PET SNAIL
WEEKLY ACTIVITY

WEEK OF..........................
DATE..............................

- Wash snail's shell
- Weigh snail and record
- Wipe tank sides and lid
- Wash cuttle fish bone if dirty

FEW MONTHLY ACTIVITY

- Top up substrate
- Wash & top up moss

TO DO
1.
2.
3.
4.
5.
6.

SHOPPING LIST

NOTES:

MY PET SNAIL
DAILY ACTIVITY

WEEK OF .... DATE..........................

SUN MON TUE WED THU FRI SUN

- Feed snail
- Fresh water
- Check a calcium source
- Remove poop
- Remove rotting food
- Spray the tank with water.
- Check the temperature

HIGHLY OF THE WEEK:

MY PET SNAIL
WEEKLY ACTIVITY

WEEK OF..........................
DATE................................

- Wash snail's shell
- Weigh snail and record
- Wipe tank sides and lid
- Wash cuttle fish bone if dirty

FEW MONTHLY ACTIVITY

- Top up substrate
- Wash & top up moss

TO DO
1.
2.
3.
4.
5.
6.

SHOPPING LIST

NOTES:

MY PET SNAIL
DAILY ACTIVITY

WEEK OF ……… DATE…………………………

SUN MON TUE WED THU FRI SUN

	Activity	S	M	T	W	T	F	S
	Feed snail	○	○	○	○	○	○	○
	Fresh water	○	○	○	○	○	○	○
	Check a calcium source	○	○	○	○	○	○	○
	Remove poop	○	○	○	○	○	○	○
	Remove rotting food	○	○	○	○	○	○	○
	Spray the tank with water.	○	○	○	○	○	○	○
	Check the temperature	○	○	○	○	○	○	○

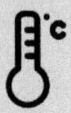

HIGHLY OF THE WEEK:

MY PET SNAIL
WEEKLY ACTIVITY

WEEK OF..........................
DATE..............................

- Wash snail's shell
- Weigh snail and record
- Wipe tank sides and lid
- Wash cuttle fish bone if dirty

FEW MONTHLY ACTIVITY

- Top up substrate
- Wash & top up moss

TO DO
1.
2.
3.
4.
5.
6.

SHOPPING LIST

NOTES:

MY PET SNAIL
DAILY ACTIVITY

WEEK OF .... DATE ....

SUN MON TUE WED THU FRI SUN

- Feed snail
- Fresh water
- Check a calcium source
- Remove poop
- Remove rotting food
- Spray the tank with water.
- Check the temperature

HIGHLY OF THE WEEK:

MY PET SNAIL
WEEKLY ACTIVITY

WEEK OF..........................
DATE..............................

- Wash snail's shell
- Weigh snail and record
- Wipe tank sides and lid
- Wash cuttle fish bone if dirty

FEW MONTHLY ACTIVITY

- Top up substrate
- Wash & top up moss

TO DO
1.
2.
3.
4.
5.
6.

SHOPPING LIST

NOTES:

MY PET SNAIL
DAILY ACTIVITY

WEEK OF .... DATE ....

SUN MON TUE WED THU FRI SUN

- Feed snail
- Fresh water
- Check a calcium source
- Remove poop
- Remove rotting food
- Spray the tank with water.
- Check the temperature

HIGHLY OF THE WEEK:

MY PET SNAIL
WEEKLY ACTIVITY

WEEK OF..........................
DATE..............................

- Wash snail's shell
- Weigh snail and record
- Wipe tank sides and lid
- Wash cuttle fish bone if dirty

FEW MONTHLY ACTIVITY

- Top up substrate
- Wash & top up moss

TO DO
1.
2.
3.
4.
5.
6.

SHOPPING LIST

NOTES:

MY PET SNAIL
DAILY ACTIVITY

WEEK OF .... DATE..........................
SUN MON TUE WED THU FRI SUN

- Feed snail
- Fresh water
- Check a calcium source
- Remove poop
- Remove rotting food
- Spray the tank with water.
- Check the temperature

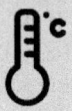

HIGHLY OF THE WEEK:

MY PET SNAIL
WEEKLY ACTIVITY

WEEK OF..........................
DATE..............................

- Wash snail's shell
- Weigh snail and record
- Wipe tank sides and lid
- Wash cuttle fish bone if dirty

FEW MONTHLY ACTIVITY

- Top up substrate
- Wash & top up moss

TO DO
1.
2.
3.
4.
5.
6.

SHOPPING LIST

NOTES:

MY PET SNAIL
DAILY ACTIVITY

WEEK OF .... DATE..........................

SUN MON TUE WED THU FRI SUN

- Feed snail
- Fresh water
- Check a calcium source
- Remove poop
- Remove rotting food
- Spray the tank with water.
- Check the temperature

HIGHLY OF THE WEEK:

MY PET SNAIL
WEEKLY ACTIVITY

WEEK OF..........................
DATE...............................

- Wash snail's shell
- Weigh snail and record
- Wipe tank sides and lid
- Wash cuttle fish bone if dirty

FEW MONTHLY ACTIVITY

- Top up substrate
- Wash & top up moss

TO DO
1.
2.
3.
4.
5.
6.

SHOPPING LIST

NOTES:

MY PET SNAIL
DAILY ACTIVITY

WEEK OF .... DATE............................

SUN MON TUE WED THU FRI SUN

- Feed snail
- Fresh water
- Check a calcium source
- Remove poop
- Remove rotting food
- Spray the tank with water.
- Check the temperature

HIGHLY OF THE WEEK:

MY PET SNAIL

WEEK OF..........................
DATE................................

WEEKLY ACTIVITY

- Wash snail's shell
- Weigh snail and record
- Wipe tank sides and lid
- Wash cuttle fish bone if dirty

FEW MONTHLY ACTIVITY

- Top up substrate
- Wash & top up moss

TO DO
1.
2.
3.
4.
5.
6.

SHOPPING LIST

NOTES:

MY PET SNAIL
DAILY ACTIVITY

WEEK OF .... DATE ....

SUN MON TUE WED THU FRI SUN

	Activity	S	M	T	W	T	F	S
	Feed snail	○	○	○	○	○	○	○
	Fresh water	○	○	○	○	○	○	○
	Check a calcium source	○	○	○	○	○	○	○
	Remove poop	○	○	○	○	○	○	○
	Remove rotting food	○	○	○	○	○	○	○
	Spray the tank with water.	○	○	○	○	○	○	○
	Check the temperature	○	○	○	○	○	○	○

HIGHLY OF THE WEEK:

MY PET SNAIL
WEEKLY ACTIVITY

WEEK OF..........................
DATE................................

- Wash snail's shell
- Weigh snail and record
- Wipe tank sides and lid
- Wash cuttle fish bone if dirty

FEW MONTHLY ACTIVITY

- Top up substrate
- Wash & top up moss

TO DO
1.
2.
3.
4.
5.
6.

SHOPPING LIST

NOTES:

MY PET SNAIL
DAILY ACTIVITY

WEEK OF .... DATE........................

SUN MON TUE WED THU FRI SUN

- Feed snail
- Fresh water
- Check a calcium source
- Remove poop
- Remove rotting food
- Spray the tank with water.
- Check the temperature

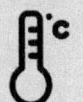

HIGHLY OF THE WEEK:

MY PET SNAIL
WEEKLY ACTIVITY

WEEK OF..........................
DATE................................

- Wash snail's shell
- Weigh snail and record
- Wipe tank sides and lid
- Wash cuttle fish bone if dirty

FEW MONTHLY ACTIVITY

- Top up substrate
- Wash & top up moss

TO DO
1.
2.
3.
4.
5.
6.

SHOPPING LIST

NOTES:

MY PET SNAIL
DAILY ACTIVITY

WEEK OF .... DATE..........................

SUN MON TUE WED THU FRI SUN

- Feed snail
- Fresh water
- Check a calcium source
- Remove poop
- Remove rotting food
- Spray the tank with water.
- Check the temperature

HIGHLY OF THE WEEK:

MY PET SNAIL
WEEKLY ACTIVITY

WEEK OF..........................
DATE..............................

- Wash snail's shell
- Weigh snail and record
- Wipe tank sides and lid
- Wash cuttle fish bone if dirty

FEW MONTHLY ACTIVITY

- Top up substrate
- Wash & top up moss

TO DO
1.
2.
3.
4.
5.
6.

SHOPPING LIST

NOTES:

MY PET SNAIL
DAILY ACTIVITY

WEEK OF .... DATE..........................

SUN MON TUE WED THU FRI SUN

	Feed snail	● ● ● ● ● ● ●
	Fresh water	● ● ● ● ● ● ●
	Check a calcium source	● ● ● ● ● ● ●
	Remove poop	● ● ● ● ● ● ●
	Remove rotting food	● ● ● ● ● ● ●
	Spray the tank with water.	● ● ● ● ● ● ●
	Check the temperature	● ● ● ● ● ● ●

HIGHLY OF THE WEEK:

MY PET SNAIL
WEEKLY ACTIVITY

WEEK OF........................
DATE..............................

- Wash snail's shell
- Weigh snail and record
- Wipe tank sides and lid
- Wash cuttle fish bone if dirty

FEW MONTHLY ACTIVITY

- Top up substrate
- Wash & top up moss

TO DO
1.
2.
3.
4.
5.
6.

SHOPPING LIST

NOTES:

MY PET SNAIL
DAILY ACTIVITY

WEEK OF .... DATE..........................

SUN MON TUE WED THU FRI SUN

	Activity							
	Feed snail	○	○	○	○	○	○	○
	Fresh water	○	○	○	○	○	○	○
	Check a calcium source	○	○	○	○	○	○	○
	Remove poop	○	○	○	○	○	○	○
	Remove rotting food	○	○	○	○	○	○	○
	Spray the tank with water.	○	○	○	○	○	○	○
	Check the temperature	○	○	○	○	○	○	○

HIGHLY OF THE WEEK:

MY PET SNAIL
WEEKLY ACTIVITY

WEEK OF............................
DATE..................................

- Wash snail's shell
- Weigh snail and record
- Wipe tank sides and lid
- Wash cuttle fish bone if dirty

FEW MONTHLY ACTIVITY

- Top up substrate
- Wash & top up moss

TO DO
1.
2.
3.
4.
5.
6.

SHOPPING LIST

NOTES:

MY PET SNAIL
DAILY ACTIVITY

WEEK OF .... DATE..............................

SUN MON TUE WED THU FRI SUN

Icon	Activity	SUN	MON	TUE	WED	THU	FRI	SUN
🍎	Feed snail	○	○	○	○	○	○	○
💧	Fresh water	○	○	○	○	○	○	○
Ca	Check a calcium source	○	○	○	○	○	○	○
💩	Remove poop	○	○	○	○	○	○	○
🍎	Remove rotting food	○	○	○	○	○	○	○
🧴	Spray the tank with water.	○	○	○	○	○	○	○
🌡°C	Check the temperature	○	○	○	○	○	○	○

HIGHLY OF THE WEEK:

MY PET SNAIL
WEEKLY ACTIVITY

WEEK OF..........................
DATE..............................

- Wash snail's shell
- Weigh snail and record
- Wipe tank sides and lid
- Wash cuttle fish bone if dirty

FEW MONTHLY ACTIVITY

- Top up substrate
- Wash & top up moss

TO DO
1.
2.
3.
4.
5.
6.

SHOPPING LIST

NOTES:

MY PET SNAIL
DAILY ACTIVITY

WEEK OF .... DATE ....

SUN MON TUE WED THU FRI SUN

	Feed snail	● ● ● ● ● ● ●
	Fresh water	● ● ● ● ● ● ●
	Check a calcium source	● ● ● ● ● ● ●
	Remove poop	● ● ● ● ● ● ●
	Remove rotting food	● ● ● ● ● ● ●
	Spray the tank with water.	● ● ● ● ● ● ●
	Check the temperature	● ● ● ● ● ● ●

HIGHLY OF THE WEEK:

MY PET SNAIL

WEEKLY ACTIVITY

WEEK OF..........................
DATE..............................

- Wash snail's shell
- Weigh snail and record
- Wipe tank sides and lid
- Wash cuttle fish bone if dirty

FEW MONTHLY ACTIVITY

- Top up substrate
- Wash & top up moss

TO DO
1.
2.
3.
4.
5.
6.

SHOPPING LIST

NOTES:

MY PET SNAIL
DAILY ACTIVITY

WEEK OF .... DATE............................

SUN MON TUE WED THU FRI SUN

- Feed snail
- Fresh water
- Check a calcium source
- Remove poop
- Remove rotting food
- Spray the tank with water.
- Check the temperature

HIGHLY OF THE WEEK:

MY PET SNAIL

WEEK OF........................

WEEKLY ACTIVITY

DATE............................

- Wash snail's shell
- Weigh snail and record
- Wipe tank sides and lid
- Wash cuttle fish bone if dirty

FEW MONTHLY ACTIVITY

- Top up substrate
- Wash & top up moss

TO DO
1.
2.
3.
4.
5.
6.

SHOPPING LIST

NOTES:

MY PET SNAIL
DAILY ACTIVITY

WEEK OF .... DATE ....

SUN MON TUE WED THU FRI SUN

- Feed snail
- Fresh water
- Check a calcium source
- Remove poop
- Remove rotting food
- Spray the tank with water.
- Check the temperature

HIGHLY OF THE WEEK:

MY PET SNAIL
WEEKLY ACTIVITY

WEEK OF..........................
DATE..............................

TO DO
1.
2.
3.
4.
5.
6.

- Wash snail's shell
- Weigh snail and record
- Wipe tank sides and lid
- Wash cuttle fish bone if dirty

FEW MONTHLY ACTIVITY

- Top up substrate
- Wash & top up moss

SHOPPING LIST

NOTES:

MY PET SNAIL
DAILY ACTIVITY

WEEK OF .... DATE............................

		SUN	MON	TUE	WED	THU	FRI	SUN
	Feed snail	○	○	○	○	○	○	○
	Fresh water	○	○	○	○	○	○	○
	Check a calcium source	○	○	○	○	○	○	○
	Remove poop	○	○	○	○	○	○	○
	Remove rotting food	○	○	○	○	○	○	○
	Spray the tank with water.	○	○	○	○	○	○	○
	Check the temperature	○	○	○	○	○	○	○

HIGHLY OF THE WEEK:

MY PET SNAIL
WEEKLY ACTIVITY

WEEK OF..........................
DATE..............................

- Wash snail's shell
- Weigh snail and record
- Wipe tank sides and lid
- Wash cuttle fish bone if dirty

FEW MONTHLY ACTIVITY

- Top up substrate
- Wash & top up moss

TO DO
1.
2.
3.
4.
5.
6.

SHOPPING LIST

NOTES:

MY PET SNAIL
DAILY ACTIVITY

WEEK OF .... DATE..........................
SUN MON TUE WED THU FRI SUN

- Feed snail
- Fresh water
- Check a calcium source
- Remove poop
- Remove rotting food
- Spray the tank with water.
- Check the temperature

HIGHLY OF THE WEEK:

MY PET SNAIL

WEEKLY ACTIVITY

WEEK OF..........................
DATE..............................

- Wash snail's shell
- Weigh snail and record
- Wipe tank sides and lid
- Wash cuttle fish bone if dirty

FEW MONTHLY ACTIVITY

- Top up substrate
- Wash & top up moss

TO DO
1.
2.
3.
4.
5.
6.

SHOPPING LIST

NOTES:

MY PET SNAIL
DAILY ACTIVITY

WEEK OF .... DATE............................

SUN MON TUE WED THU FRI SUN

	Activity	Sun	Mon	Tue	Wed	Thu	Fri	Sun
🍎	Feed snail	○	○	○	○	○	○	○
💧	Fresh water	○	○	○	○	○	○	○
Ca	Check a calcium source	○	○	○	○	○	○	○
💩	Remove poop	○	○	○	○	○	○	○
	Remove rotting food	○	○	○	○	○	○	○
	Spray the tank with water.	○	○	○	○	○	○	○
🌡°C	Check the temperature	○	○	○	○	○	○	○

HIGHLY OF THE WEEK:

MY PET SNAIL
WEEKLY ACTIVITY

WEEK OF..........................
DATE..............................

- Wash snail's shell
- Weigh snail and record
- Wipe tank sides and lid
- Wash cuttle fish bone if dirty

FEW MONTHLY ACTIVITY

- Top up substrate
- Wash & top up moss

TO DO
1.
2.
3.
4.
5.
6.

SHOPPING LIST

NOTES:

MY PET SNAIL
DAILY ACTIVITY

WEEK OF .... DATE............................

SUN MON TUE WED THU FRI SUN

🍎	Feed snail	○ ○ ○ ○ ○ ○ ○
💧	Fresh water	○ ○ ○ ○ ○ ○ ○
Ca	Check a calcium source	○ ○ ○ ○ ○ ○ ○
💩	Remove poop	○ ○ ○ ○ ○ ○ ○
	Remove rotting food	○ ○ ○ ○ ○ ○ ○
	Spray the tank with water.	○ ○ ○ ○ ○ ○ ○
🌡°C	Check the temperature	○ ○ ○ ○ ○ ○ ○

HIGHLY OF THE WEEK:

MY PET SNAIL
WEEKLY ACTIVITY

WEEK OF..........................
DATE..............................

- Wash snail's shell
- Weigh snail and record
- Wipe tank sides and lid
- Wash cuttle fish bone if dirty

FEW MONTHLY ACTIVITY

- Top up substrate
- Wash & top up moss

TO DO
1.
2.
3.
4.
5.
6.

SHOPPING LIST

NOTES:

MY PET SNAIL
DAILY ACTIVITY

WEEK OF .... DATE............................
SUN MON TUE WED THU FRI SUN

	Activity	SUN	MON	TUE	WED	THU	FRI	SUN
	Feed snail	○	○	○	○	○	○	○
	Fresh water	○	○	○	○	○	○	○
	Check a calcium source	○	○	○	○	○	○	○
	Remove poop	○	○	○	○	○	○	○
	Remove rotting food	○	○	○	○	○	○	○
	Spray the tank with water.	○	○	○	○	○	○	○
	Check the temperature	○	○	○	○	○	○	○

HIGHLY OF THE WEEK:

MY PET SNAIL
WEEKLY ACTIVITY

WEEK OF..........................
DATE..............................

- Wash snail's shell
- Weigh snail and record
- Wipe tank sides and lid
- Wash cuttle fish bone if dirty

FEW MONTHLY ACTIVITY

- Top up substrate
- Wash & top up moss

TO DO
1.
2.
3.
4.
5.
6.

SHOPPING LIST

NOTES:

MY PET SNAIL
DAILY ACTIVITY

WEEK OF .... DATE..........................

SUN MON TUE WED THU FRI SUN

	Activity	S	M	T	W	T	F	S
	Feed snail	○	○	○	○	○	○	○
	Fresh water	○	○	○	○	○	○	○
	Check a calcium source	○	○	○	○	○	○	○
	Remove poop	○	○	○	○	○	○	○
	Remove rotting food	○	○	○	○	○	○	○
	Spray the tank with water.	○	○	○	○	○	○	○
	Check the temperature	○	○	○	○	○	○	○

HIGHLY OF THE WEEK:

MY PET SNAIL
WEEKLY ACTIVITY

WEEK OF..........................
DATE..............................

- Wash snail's shell
- Weigh snail and record
- Wipe tank sides and lid
- Wash cuttle fish bone if dirty

FEW MONTHLY ACTIVITY

- Top up substrate
- Wash & top up moss

TO DO
1.
2.
3.
4.
5.
6.

SHOPPING LIST

NOTES:

Printed in Great Britain
by Amazon